Anthology

Ace it! TUTORING ℠ Reading

content provided
by Houghton Mifflin Harcourt
Supplemental Publishers, Inc.

Photo Acknowledgements: p.3 (Duke) ©Hulton-Deutsch Collection/CORBIS; p.3 (surfboard) ©Ron Chapple/Getty Images; p.4 (Duke) ©Hulton Archive/Getty Images; p.4 (surfboards 1930,1930s,1960s) ©Primedia Surfer Archives; p.4 (surfboard today) ©Ron Chapple/Getty Images; p.9 ©Franz Lating/Minden Pictures; p.10 ©Digital Visions/Getty Images; p.11 ©Tui DeRoy/Minden Pictures; p. pp.17-20 ©Photo Courtesy William Wegman; p.26 ©Roger Ressmeyer/CORBIS; p.27 ©Mimmo Jodice/CORBIS; p.28 ©Mimmo Jodice/CORBIS; p.30 ©Peter Menzel Photography; p.31 ©Michael Freeman/CORBIS; p.39 ©COR-BIS; p.40 (Golden Gate) ©CORBIS; p.40 (Gateway) ©Photodisc/Getty Images; p.40 (Petronas) ©CORBIS.

Additional photography by Comstock Royalty Free; ImageState Royalty Free; Photos.com Royalty Free; Photodisc/Getty Royalty Free; PictureQuest Royalty Free and Royalty-Free/CORBIS.

ISBN 0-4190-2663-1

Printed in the United States of America
9 10 11 1420 14 13 12
4500351347

Contents

Level F
Comprehension

LET'S GO SURFING!

Imagine yourself a hundred yards from a glittering sandy beach. Brilliant sunshine fills a crystal clear sky and warms your back. Light dances off the water that surrounds you. You're racing toward the shore at close to 50 miles (80.5 kilometers) per hour. There is only a thin board beneath your feet to separate you from the powerful ocean. A towering wave threatens to **envelop** you, but you stay just ahead of it. Shifting your weight from one foot to the other, you **maneuver** the board through the smooth water below the **cresting** wave. You're surfing!

Riding the Waves

Surfing is a water sport performed mostly in the ocean, although some committed surfers try to find waves in large lakes. Surfers use rigid boards to glide across the smooth sloping parts of waves. First, they lie on the boards to paddle out beyond the breaking waves. Then surfers turn to face the beach. Next, they kneel on the boards. Finally, they stand as the wave begins to rise. Surfers ride the wave toward the shore, **prolonging** the ride by moving across the face of the wave.

Skilled surfers use balance and timing to perform an **array** of different tricks. Today's surfers show their skills in two main ways. One type of surfer participates in organized competitions. Judges rank tricks, length of ride, and even grace while riding. This competitive surfing has been accepted by the International Olympic Committee.

Another type of surfer views the sport as a purely personal way to get close to nature. These surfers avoid the competition **circuit** and search the globe for the perfect wave to enjoy in private. You may not be able to admire these surfers' moves in competition, but you can often find videos or magazines that showcase their skills.

Duke Kahanamoku

A Royal History

Surfing traces its history to the early Polynesians, including those living in what is now Hawaii. Some experts believe that Hawaiian kings surfed in their religious ceremonies. Others say that both kings and citizens enjoyed surfing as a sport. In any case, early surfing dates back at least to the 15th century. Change came in the 1800s, however, when large numbers of Europeans arrived in Hawaii. Some Europeans did not like the sport and tried to **eliminate** it.

In 1920, however, a young Hawaiian named Duke Kahanamoku helped bring the sport back by founding a surfing club. Duke was no ordinary Hawaiian. He was an Olympic swimming champion, grandson of a high chief, and an accomplished surfer. Duke gained recognition for his sport by traveling as far away as Australia to show off his skills. Surfing also grew in popularity as more and more people visited Hawaii for its sunny weather and lovely beaches. These tourists brought news of surfing back to the mainland.

Then, during the 1950s and 1960s, the **identity** of the surfer began to change. Surfers developed their own language. You could spot surfers by their suntans and the casual clothes they wore. Before long, surf music and movies helped bring surfing style to young people all over the United States.

Surfer Talk

360: a trick where the surfer does a complete turn

hang ten: a trick where all ten toes rest on the nose of the surfboard

ono: Hawaiian word for "great"

ripping: doing amazing tricks on a wave

wipe out: when a surfer is knocked off of a surfboard by a wave

the zone: area inside or between waves when they are breaking

The Changing Surfboard

The early Hawaiians surfed on wooden boards that were 18 feet (5.5 meters) long. Duke Kahanamoku's boards were 8 to 10 feet (2.4 to 3 meters) long and solid wood. These surfboards were heavy and hard to handle.

However, over time, surfboards improved. In the 1930s, a surfer looking for speed developed a hollow board. The surfer also added a fin to help him guide the board. Even this board still weighed 60 to 70 pounds (27.2 to 31.8 kilograms)!

It wasn't long before lighter woods and plastics led to the *malibu*, a board weighing just 20 pounds (9 kilograms). The *malibu* **transformed** surfing. Now surfers could really steer their boards. They could move around to do tricks. Even carrying a surfboard became much easier. This encouraged surfers to travel in search of "perfect" waves. Most of all, *malibus* made learning to surf easier. This brought more and more people to the sport.

Today's surfboards are very different from those used by the first surfers. The new boards are built mostly of plastic. They are shorter and usually more narrow than the early boards. A typical board is now about 6 feet (1.8 meters) long and weighs about 5 pounds (2.3 kilograms). Also, most boards now have three fins as well as shaped edges to make steering more **precise**. If you ever take to the waves, you'll enjoy these improvements. They'll keep you ahead of that huge wave.

Duke Kahanamoku poses with his huge surfboard.

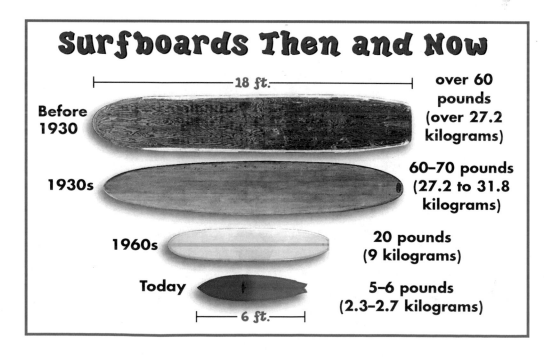

Surfboards Then and Now

Before 1930	18 ft.	**over 60 pounds (over 27.2 kilograms)**
1930s		**60–70 pounds (27.2 to 31.8 kilograms)**
1960s		**20 pounds (9 kilograms)**
Today	6 ft.	**5–6 pounds (2.3–2.7 kilograms)**

LOST!

Matt was burning with **anticipation**. Today he and his sister Lynn were finally going to scale Canfield Peak. He'd wanted to tackle the climb since he was six years old. Now that Lynn was in college and Matt was in middle school, Matt's mom had agreed that they could make the hike alone.

Matt banged on Lynn's door. "Hey, let's go before the day disappears," he called.

Lynn and Matt drove to the base of Canfield Peak. With their gear on their backs, they began the **strenuous** climb. At first the time flew by, but as they came closer to the peak, the climb became more and more difficult. After about four tough hours, they reached the peak. The sun blazed high in the sky and the hikers were hot, dusty, and exhausted. But the view was worth the hard work. It was absolutely beautiful and they could see for miles around.

"You did it!" exclaimed Lynn with enthusiasm. "You're an awesome hiker, for a 12 year-old."

"What do you mean, for a 12 year-old? I'm a good hiker for any age," **retorted** Matt. "Let's head back down. That took a lot longer than we thought it would."

After stopping for a snack to **refresh** themselves, Lynn and Matt started back down. Lynn pointed out sights they'd overlooked on the way up. Soon, the hikers came to a fork in the trail.

"Which way, Lynn?" asked Matt, looking puzzled.

"This way," said Lynn, pointing to the right. "I'm almost certain Dad and I turned right here when we did this last year."

They hiked on at a steady pace. However, as the sun sank into the mountains and the temperature dropped, the trail became unfamiliar. They hadn't passed another hiker for miles. There were twists, turns, and decisions to be made every hundred yards. They constantly asked each other, "Right or left? Left or right?"

After an hour of wandering and discussing trail options, Lynn had to admit it. They were lost.

"It's late and almost completely dark," worried Lynn aloud. "I don't think we should keep hiking when we can't see properly. We're just getting more and more lost. I even feel as if we're walking up, not down."

"I think you're right," said Matt. "We've got to come up with a plan and use some **survival** skills."

They traced their steps back to a small cave that was near a clearing they had recently passed. "This might do the trick," Lynn said, **surveying** the cave.

But Matt shook his head. "I don't think we should stay here," he said. "Look at those tracks leading in and out. There could be wild animals living here. We don't want any unexpected visitors in the middle of the night!"

Then Lynn spotted some large rocks just a few feet off the path. The two looked carefully and discovered a sheltered space between one large rock and a smaller one leaning up against it. "It doesn't look like there are any wild animals in here," Lynn said. "But I bet it is large enough for the two of us to sleep in."

"And small enough to trap our body heat," said Matt. "Now let's go find some branches to help keep us warm."

"Wow, Matt, I'm impressed! I never knew that you were so **resourceful**," Lynn marveled.

The two worked together and soon found enough leafy limbs to cover the opening between the rocks. They filled in the cracks with some leaves and small branches, then added some moss for more protection. The wind was becoming fierce, but it was warm and toasty inside their temporary shelter.

"I think we'll be okay without a fire for the night," said Lynn. "Plus, with this wind and all the dry leaves around the area, it would probably cause more harm than good."

"It's really not that bad in here," said Matt. "Let's divide our food and water. And thank Mom for packing such large lunches."

Huddled together under the leaves and branches, the two sang songs to pass the time and keep calm as the sounds of the mountain crept into their shelter. Coyotes howled, owls hooted, and the wind blew the trees, making them creak and moan.

In spite of their fear, they couldn't help but become **drowsy**. They were worn out from the climb and their efforts to make a decent shelter. Matt grabbed the jacket he'd wisely brought along and draped it across his sister and himself. Soon they fell asleep.

When Lynn awoke, it was morning and Matt was outside the shelter. She rubbed her eyes and tried to focus on what he was doing.

"I'm trying to signal for help, Lynn," he said. "I'm using the cap of the metal thermos to reflect the sunlight to the base of the mountain. It works almost like a flashlight."

Watching him in the dawn light, Lynn realized that her baby brother had turned into an **extraordinary** young man. After what seemed like hours, Matt thought he heard some distant calls.

"Hey, Lynn," shouted Matt, "I think the searchers are headed this way. Lend me your incredibly loud voice to answer their calls."

They hollered, "We're over here!" until they grew **hoarse**. Finally, the searchers emerged from the trees, nearly crashing into Lynn and Matt, who ran full tilt with joy and relief. It was their parents!

The Long Road Home:
The Life Cycle and Migration of Green Sea Turtles

Dozens of tiny green sea turtles paw quickly at the sand all around them. They've just hatched from their soft eggs and lie buried in a sandy nest. To survive, they must scratch their way to the surface and crawl to the sea. Working as a group, the baby turtles finally emerge from the nest into the cool night air.

The mother turtle is gone. She left the nest some sixty days earlier after laying the eggs. Now the **hatchlings** face many **hazards** as they struggle to stay alive. First, they must figure out where the sea is. Some scientists think they do this by looking for the brightest horizon. Next, the hatchlings must reach the sea before they dry out in the sun. They also may **encounter** crabs or birds who want to eat them.

9

Growing Up

Because their mother is gone, baby turtles that reach the ocean will swim unprotected from sharks and other large fish. With such dangers, it takes great effort and **persistence** to reach giant beds of seaweed far offshore. The seaweed offers warm waters, food, and protection from enemies.

Adrift and floating in weeds, the baby turtles spend several years eating and growing. They eat worms, baby crabs, sea insects, and plants. Then they find their way to feeding grounds that are closer to shore. For several more years, the teenaged turtles eat and grow their way toward being full-sized. It can take 20 years or more to become an adult. As a result of many challenges on the road to adulthood, just one in one thousand baby sea turtles actually grows to be an adult turtle.

Most green sea turtle feeding grounds are in warm, coastal waters. Adult turtles spend their days eating sea plants and resting. They sleep beneath the safety of shore rocks.

When fully mature, these green sea turtles may be about 3 feet (.9 meters) long and weigh 300 pounds (136 kilograms). Size and strength will help the turtles **evade** enemies on yet another journey.

Journey to the Nest

Every few years, adult green sea turtles swim from their feeding grounds to nesting areas that are far away. When mating time approaches, both male and female turtles begin the long journey back to the nesting site. Amazingly, the turtles can **navigate** their way to very specific nesting sites, often the same site where they themselves were born. Some green sea turtles, for example, feed and spend much of their adult lives on the coasts of South America. But they lay their eggs on Ascension (uh SEN shuhn) Island far out in the Atlantic Ocean. To get to the nesting area, the turtles must make a journey of nearly 1400 miles (2200 kilometers).

Scientists are not certain how sea turtles find their way when they travel such long distances. One new theory suggests that turtles can sense the magnetic forces from the North and South Poles. By sensing these forces, the turtles determine where the nesting sites are on the globe.

Once they reach the nesting grounds, mating begins in the waters near shore. When they are ready to lay their eggs, the females head to shore. Night often shields the green sea turtles from predators as they climb the beach. Each female turtle has her own favorite spot that she returns to again and again.

In a dry area safe from the surf, the mother turtle digs a deep nesting hole. It is **oblong**, shaped a bit like a drop of water with a wider than usual tip. She then begins to deposit her eggs. She lays two or three at a time, a total of 80 to 120 eggs, deep into the pit. Finally, she covers the nest with sand. She may return to the same spot four or five more times that season to lay more eggs. Then she heads back to her feeding ground to begin the cycle again.

After laying her eggs, the mother turtle returns to sea.

Protecting the Turtles

Green sea turtles are ancient animals. They have been around for millions of years. Today, however, they face a serious danger. Feeding and nesting grounds have been disturbed or destroyed, often by human activities. In some places, other sea turtles are already **extinct**. People are afraid that the green sea turtle may follow.

A Sea Turtle Migration Pattern

ATLANTIC OCEAN

Nesting Site

February

November   June

Florida

N
W   E
S

Scientists can use satellites to track the path of a sea turtle.

One way to protect green sea turtles is to learn more about them, their habits, and how they have changed over the years. The best way to find out about green sea turtles of long ago is by looking at their **fossils**. To find out about the behavior of the turtles today, scientists can study their patterns of migration. They place small metal tags on female turtles at their nesting sites. They can track the turtles' paths by reading the tags at feeding sites or even by finding lost tags. Scientists also use space satellites to track turtles. The satellites locate signals sent by tracking devices that are attached to the turtles.

Ordinary people can do their part to protect green sea turtles and other animals, too. One way is to keep the world's beaches and oceans clean. Studies show that many turtles die from accidentally eating plastic and other garbage found on or near beaches. Another way to protect the sea turtles is to keep their nesting grounds safe so hatchlings have a greater chance of survival. Finally, people can work together to prevent illegal hunting of the turtles for their meat and shells. Through these efforts, green sea turtles will hopefully be around for a long time to come.

THE BIG SPLASH!

"Have fun guys, and stay in the raft!" my mom called from her group. "And Jenny," she added with a wink, "keep an eye on your father."

The whitewater rafting guides had organized all the rafters in groups for equal weight **distribution**. They had split up some family members. My mom, my older brother Jeremy, and a bunch of people we'd never met were in one raft. In my raft, there was my dad, my younger brother Todd, a couple on their honeymoon, two friends named Chen and Percy, and Percy's dad. Our guide's name was Marisol. While carrying the raft toward the Colorado River, Marisol barked orders as other guides came around to **douse** everyone with cold river water.

"You won't melt from the cold water," Marisol laughed as we yelped with surprise. "Better now than later. You'll have to get used to it. This is a wet ride!"

Everyone cringed at the cold water, but we were determined to act like real rafters. Marisol divided us on the two sides of the raft and demonstrated how to secure ourselves with our feet.

"Todd, you'll be stationed back here with me so you can squeeze down all the way into the raft when the going gets rough. That's the safest place for a younger person," Marisol reassured my doubtful dad. "Okay! Are we ready to tackle the rapids?"

Everyone nodded, though I felt pretty **incompetent** about rafting. I glanced repeatedly at Todd, who was perched next to Marisol and had a rope to hold on to because his feet didn't reach the floor. I knew he was a bit nervous, but hoped he'd have fun anyway.

We were off, and quickly felt the raft's **buoyancy** as it hit the river's water and began to float. Our "put-in point" was a stretch of calm, peaceful water that gave us a chance to practice newly learned directions such as "Everyone forward paddle one!" or "Back paddle on the left two, forward on the right three!" At first we had trouble keeping the raft going forward, but soon we caught on and began working like a well-oiled machine.

Our new companion, Percy, pointed to the riverbank where a pair of mountain goats stood silently watching us. Everyone whispered "Wow!" with awe in their voices. The sun blazed hot in the cloudless western sky and I thought to myself how peaceful this seemed. Then, little by little, the raft sped up.

"Paddle! Paddle!" Marisol yelled as we cruised on to rougher waters.

"Our first rapid is just ahead," explained Marisol. "It's called 'The Ankle Bone' because we'll travel around a bend in the river shaped like an ankle bone. Everybody remember to paddle on my commands. We need to steer this raft through the rapids. Okay, now everyone check that your feet are secure. Ready . . . forward paddle two!"

I felt my heart rate soar as the sounds of the rapids grew louder and angrier. We all hollered shouts of encouragement as the other rafts plunged into the rapids ahead of us, bucking **frantically** up and down.

When it was our turn, Dad grabbed Todd, and I braced myself for **impact** as the raft headed for the rocks. Water sprayed high into the air around us, splashing us all. Over the rushing noise of the water and the shouts of our group, Marisol calmly instructed us, "Two forward on the left, and now two more." Gradually, the water slowed and the raft settled.

"Awesome!" Todd yelled to me. Rafting had him hooked for sure. "Are there more rapids? Are there more?" he asked Marisol excitedly.

"See," replied Marisol, "you're a river rat after all. Don't worry, you'll get plenty of amazing rides today because the river is high and the water is running fast. But we can't **endanger** your dad, right?" she continued, with a sly grin in my direction.

"I'm ready," I said, hungry for more. "Bring it on." Then I heard more roaring water up ahead.

"Okay folks," shouted Marisol. "This is a big one called 'The Hole,' for obvious reasons. The water wants to suck our raft right down into that hole and we've got to paddle hard to keep on course."

In an instant, it seemed as if we were headed over a **precipice**. The raft dropped down into a narrow stretch of water with steep rocks looming above on all sides. Towering waves crashed all around us as the currents bounced the raft around like a toy. Our raft tipped until it felt like it was almost straight up in the air. I was sure we were about to overturn.

Marisol hollered "High side! High side!" and we all scrambled to weigh down the **teetering** high side. We hung in the air for a moment that felt like a lifetime, and then the raft found its balance again. Once we were stable, Dad grabbed Todd and **embraced** him, asking, "Are you okay? Were you scared?"

"Are you kidding, Dad? This is great, except for you grabbing me every two seconds," he said. I rolled my eyes and grinned at Marisol. We both knew who the scared one was.

As we settled back in our seats, Marisol sounded the call once again. "Paddle! Paddle! Paddle!" she bellowed. I didn't know about my dad, but I was ready for more!

WILLIAM WEGMAN:
A DOG'S BEST FRIEND

Have you ever taken a photograph? Imagine being a photographer and taking pictures all the time. Perhaps you would take pictures of beautiful places, exotic animals, or even famous people.

If you're anything like William Wegman, though, you might photograph something less traditional— like dogs that have been dressed to look like people! William Wegman is an artist who has made a career of doing just that. His work has been **exhibited** in museums and art galleries all over the world. Since he started photographing his dogs in 1970, he has become quite famous. So have his dogs!

An Artist Gets His Start

William Wegman was born in 1943 in Holyoke, Massachusetts. As a boy, William loved to draw and paint. When he was older, he decided to go to art school. William studied art at the Massachusetts College of Art and at the University of Illinois. There he learned all about painting and drawing.

Soon William finished school. He became a **professor** and taught painting in Wisconsin. During this time, however, he became interested in more **contemporary** ways of making art. He was excited by the **media** of film and photography. William experimented with both.

In 1970, William and his wife, Christine, moved from Wisconsin to California. They decided to get a dog once they had moved to their new home. They had heard that Weimaraners (WY muh RAH nuhrz) were good dogs. They answered a newspaper ad from someone selling Weimaraner puppies. That's when they got their first Weimaraner.

William named his new dog Man Ray after a famous photographer. Soon, he discovered that Man Ray was comfortable in front of the camera. He thought Man Ray would make a good subject for some photographs. Fortunately, he decided to try some of his wacky ideas.

Photography Courtesy of William Wegman

New Ideas

In the beginning, William photographed Man Ray doing normal dog activities such as eating, sleeping, and chewing on things. But soon William found that he could put Man Ray in different settings, with different props, to create scenes for his photographs. He also discovered that his dog was an enthusiastic model. An unusual **collaboration** was born between the two of them.

Man Ray was the star of William Wegman's many photographs and videos for twelve years. Then, in 1982, Man Ray died of cancer. William was **reluctant** to photograph dogs again. But in 1986, he began to work with another Weimaraner named Fay Ray. He found that Fay Ray was also **photogenic**.

Fay Ray was the first dog William dressed in human clothing. William was in his studio one day and put Fay on a high stool, which made her look tall like a person. He covered her and the stool with an old dress. He discovered that this made the dog look like a woman standing up. William was **inspired**!

Soon Fay Ray had puppies, one of whom later had her own puppies. Now William had a whole cast of dog models, named Chundo, Crooky, Battina, and Chip, to work with. He photographed and videotaped them wearing many different costumes and playing many different roles. The resulting images were both beautiful and funny. William and his Weimaraners were a big success!

Photography Courtesy of William Wegman

Photography Courtesy of William Wegman

19

The Artist Today

Today, William Wegman's work is known throughout the world. He has used his dogs to create children's books based on stories such as *Cinderella*, *Little Red Riding Hood*, and *Mother Goose*. He has also designed alphabet cards and has made videos with his well-known pooches. He now **resides** in New York City with his wife, two children, and, of course, his dogs.

Many people wonder if William's dogs are really comfortable being dressed up and photographed. But William is gentle with his dogs. He respects each dog's personality. "Every dog is an individual," he says. "Chundo doesn't like to sit long but is most eager to work... Chip doesn't mind hats. Batty falls asleep while posing with or without costume."

William also says, "Anyone who's watched us work sees that the dogs perform **willingly**. Sometimes they're excited or enthusiastic, but they're not afraid."

Clearly, William Wegman is an unusual kind of artist. He has combined his love for making art with his love for dogs. But it's not all fun and games for William and his Weimaraners. "Despite my silly photographs," he says, "it's serious work and the dogs take it seriously."

Photography Courtesy of William Wegman

A New Land, A New Life

Malka stood at the railing of the ship as it pulled into New York Harbor. She gasped at the **breathtaking** sight of the copper statue as it sparkled in the sunlight. To Malka, the sculpture **symbolized** hope for all people, no matter what country they came from.

Malka followed the other passengers down the **gangplank** and onto the crowded dock. After the long ocean journey, she was happy to be on land again. The year was 1900, the dawn of a new century. Malka's heart pounded with fear. Could she survive in this big city after growing up in a tiny village in Russia? Malka had decided she would have to try. She stood tall and walked with determination to greet her new life.

Malka had traveled alone across the ocean to this new land. Her mother, father, two sisters, and brother were back in Russia. Her father was a tailor, but his eyesight had started to fail and he could no longer work. Her mother was forced to support the family. So far, she had made enough money for only one **passage** to America.

"You are the oldest child, Malka," her mother had said. "You will go first and make your way in America. You will live with your Aunt Irina and her family. We will think of you every day, especially when we light the candles on Friday night."

Now Malka thought about her family and she was **overcome** by a wave of sadness. She missed them so much! She longed for them to join her in America. Malka decided at that moment that she must succeed in this new country. She would learn the new language, English, as quickly as she could. She would find work as a **seamstress**. She would work day and night. She would earn enough money to send for her family. Malka would make sure that their **immigration** was easier than her own.

Malka and the other passengers filed into the largest room she had ever seen. Malka waited patiently in one line and was given a health test. When she passed that, she was sent to wait in yet another line.

Malka waited as the immigration inspector searched her suitcase. He was looking for **contraband**, items that couldn't be brought into the country. Then he looked at her papers.

"Malka is your Russian name," the inspector boomed. "You are in America now. We will call you Mary." The inspector stamped her papers and Malka was free to go.

With her aunt's address in her hand, Malka hurried out of the building. She smiled as she said the foreign name out loud to herself. *Mary* might be the name on her papers, but she would always be the same in her heart. Her name would always be *Malka*. Outside the large inspection building, a kind man who spoke Russian pointed her in the right direction. Malka walked east across Manhattan Island.

That night, Malka went to sleep in her aunt's apartment in a section of New York called the Lower East Side. The street outside her window was so noisy! At first Malka thought she would never fall asleep, but soon the warmth of the feather bed comforted her and she drifted off to sleep.

Malka soon learned that the Lower East Side was a neighborhood filled with immigrants from many parts of Eastern Europe. Apartments were crowded, with more than one family living together. Most people were poor and life was very difficult. But people were grateful to be in America. Malka loved her new neighborhood, with its friendly people all struggling together. She also loved the familiar language and foods from her homeland.

Malka found work as a seamstress and worked long hours every day. It was difficult, but Malka **persevered**. She worked hard for many months and saved her money. After awhile, she was able to open a small shop of her own. She mended clothing and made dresses and suits for people in the neighborhood. She worked quickly and charged fair prices. Soon everyone spoke of Malka, the seamstress who made wonderful clothing. Her reputation grew and many people came from other neighborhoods to have their clothing made.

One day a man wearing an expensive suit came into her shop. "I like your designs. I want you to manage my clothing factory," he told Malka. "I will pay you a very good salary."

Malka was so excited. What a **breakthrough**! Her American dream was about to come true. She would soon have enough money to bring her family to her new home.

Pompeii: The City That Disappeared

Pompeii (pahm PAY) was once a beautiful city in ancient Italy. Pompeii was built more than 2500 years ago on a plateau of lava, nestled beside the Bay of Naples in Italy. Pompeii was located less than 1 mile (1.6 kilometers) south of the majestic Mount Vesuvius (vuh SOO vee uhs).

Pompeii was built in the shape of an oval. A great wall with eight gates encircled the city. It was a popular vacation area visited by wealthy people. At the center of the city was the **forum**, which was surrounded by many large public buildings. This included an **amphitheater** that could seat the entire population of Pompeii. The population was about 20,000 people.

Then one summer, this successful city was completely wiped out.

What Happened to Pompeii?

Mount Vesuvius, which looms in the background over Pompeii, proved to be the **demise** of the once thriving city. When the city was settled, Mount Vesuvius was a **dormant** volcano. It had not erupted for hundreds of years.

Seventeen years before Pompeii was wiped out, the town was struck by a massive earthquake. This earthquake could have set in motion the event that would eventually destroy the town. It is possible that this earthquake caused major Earth changes that would lead to the eruption of Mount Vesuvius. This, however, was not known by the citizens of Pompeii.

The citizens of Pompeii and nearby towns were in the middle of a regular day in August when **catastrophe** struck. Mount Vesuvius erupted suddenly and violently without any warning.

From the moment the eruptions began, the townspeople had only minutes to escape. People were forced to run for their lives without regard for their homes or property. They fled the area, chased by falling stones and clouds of ash.

An Eyewitness to Disaster

Much of what we know of the disaster at Pompeii comes from a Roman writer named Pliny the Younger. Pliny the Younger was one of Pompeii's survivors. He wrote a letter that explained how he and his mother escaped to safety through the ash clouds and falling stones. Pliny wrote that the eruption lasted for four straight days. When it finally stopped, an estimated 2000 people were left buried under the ash and lava of the volcano.

In the **aftermath** of the eruption, only the tops of the city walls and columns rose above the waste. At first, survivors returned to try to dig out their valuables and belongings. However, later eruptions of Mount Vesuvius eventually buried the last traces of the city.

The eruption of Mount Vesuvius destroyed not only Pompeii, but other nearby cities and towns. In fact, because of the eruption, the whole geography of the area was changed. The eruption changed the path of the Sarno River. It also raised the beach that bordered the bay. As a result of these Earth changes, there was no longer any way of locating the city. Pompeii remained buried deep beneath many layers of ash for thousands of years.

These murals were found unharmed in some of Pompeii's villas.

A Window to the Past

An unbelievable discovery was made in 1748. One day, a farmer was digging in his vineyard located in the countryside of Italy. His shovel hit something hard. When he dug further, he discovered a wall. He had uncovered the long-buried city of Pompeii.

Pompeii's ruins are remarkably **intact**. This is a result of the showers of wet ashes and cinders that accompanied the eruption. These ashes and cinders formed an airtight seal. This **preserved** many structures.

As the ruins were carefully uncovered, the finest examples of ancient Roman art, buildings, and homes were revealed. In addition, the remains of some of the 2000 victims of the disaster were found in the ruins. Many victims were preserved in the same position they were in when Mount Vesuvius erupted.

Today, Pompeii is visited by many **archeologists**, as well as by tourists interested in history. The ruins provide a realistic picture of life in an ancient Italian city. Visitors are able to see the central forum and the public and private baths, typical of Roman towns. We know that Pompeii was a wealthy town because of the size of the homes. A typical **villa** had an average of forty rooms!

Archeologists are still working to uncover Pompeii piece by piece. They are preserving the details of Roman civilization for many generations to come.

This Basilica served as a courthouse, a temple, and the center of the town's government.

Creepy Crawly . . . and Delicious
Insects as Food

Believe it or not, most insects we see crawling on the ground or on our picnic blankets can be eaten. In fact, many bugs and insects are quite **nutritious**. Insects are low in fat and are good sources of protein. Insects can also be quite tasty if they are cooked properly. Many cookbooks feature insect recipes. There are even **entomology** newsletters and magazines devoted to insects as food.

You may not like the idea of eating a grasshopper or a beetle. But insects are probably better for you than the high-fat, high-salt, high-calorie diet that many people have today. Put down the fast food and get ready to pass the pest food!

What's That Fly Doing in My Soup?

Does the idea of eating creepy crawlers sound less than **appetizing** to you? Don't get scared, but did you ever notice tiny black specks in your cereal or bread? These might be flour beetles and other pests that live in **granaries**. They fall into the flour as the grain is being milled.

Did you ever notice tiny things flying around fruit in the market? Well, guess what they are? Fruit flies! Chances are you've been eating insects without even knowing it. Now that you have your feet wet, why don't you take the full plunge and taste a few delicious insect **morsels**?

If you'd like to try adding insects to your diet, it's important to know how to prepare them. What is the first step on the road to successful insect-eating? All insect food experts will tell you the same thing. Get the freshest insects you can find, and cook them before eating them.

Insects usually are not found in supermarkets. However, you can purchase insects in pet stores or bait stores. You can also catch insects in the wild.

Fried waterbugs might make a tasty appetizer.

Besides eating the whole insect, insect parts are also good to eat. You may want to begin by trying wings, legs, and eggs. Insects can make delicious main courses or make a lovely **garnish** for a festive holiday plate.

International Insect Snacks

Eating insects is not a new trend. In fact, people have been eating insects throughout history. Native Americans ate plenty of different insects long before Christopher Columbus came to America.

Today, many cultures around the world have insects in their **cuisine**. In fact, eighty percent of the world's population eats insects. In South America, people eat white beetles and ants. In Mexico, there is a particular ant that people use to make salsa. This ant is found only during the rainy season. In Algeria, people collect locusts in the desert, cook them in salt water, and dry them in the sun before eating them. In Japan, many insect items can be found on restaurant menus, such as boiled wasp **larvae** and fried grasshoppers with rice. People in West Africa eat termites and caterpillars.

Insects are not only tasty and nutritious, they are also **plentiful**. Yet why aren't people in America eating more insects today? The answer is simple. Many people think that insects are disgusting! You might agree, but imagine you were lost in the woods and it was getting dark. If you had to choose between starving and eating insects, what would you do? Who knows? You might find the crispy crunch of roasted ants to be **irresistible**.

Chocolate-covered insects could be a perfect after-school snack!

We're Having *What* for Breakfast?

Tired of the same old, boring pancakes? Here's a simple and delicious recipe for grasshopper cakes to start your day right!

Grasshopper Cakes

- one egg
- twenty fresh, cooked grasshoppers
- two cups of cornmeal
- one teaspoon of cooking oil

1. Beat the egg in a bowl. Then add the grasshoppers and stir.

2. Put the grasshopper-and-egg mixture into a paper bag filled with cornmeal.

3. Make sure that the top of the bag is closed. Then shake the bag until the insects are completely covered with cornmeal.

4. Take the mixture out of the bag and make small pancake-size cakes, using your hands.

5. Ask an adult to help you fry the cakes in a skillet with a teaspoon of cooking oil. Drain and cool the cakes on a paper towel.

6. Serve plain or with syrup, butter, or honey.

Don't Let Insects Bug You!

Do you think you will be cooking buggy recipes anytime soon? If you do, remember that insects must be gathered and prepared properly. It's best to check with a health professional, a science teacher, or a parent before you take your first creepy, crawly, crunchy bite. Happy eating!

THE STORY OF ICARUS:
A GREEK MYTH

Daedalus (DEHD uh luhs) was a clever inventor who served King Minos on the Greek island of Crete. Daedalus invented and built many wonderful things for King Minos. Daedalus's son, Icarus (IK uh ruhs), was learning his father's trade and often worked by his side. However, Icarus had a bad habit of ignoring the things his father told him.

"Don't rush," Daedalus would tell his son. "Your work will be sloppy." But Icarus would not listen to his father, and Daedalus would have to undo his son's mistakes.

Among the things Daedalus created for King Minos was a **labyrinth**. It was an **intricate** maze that twisted and turned in many directions. The labyrinth was built to contain the fierce Minotaur (MIN uh taur), a beast that was half-man and half-bull. The king prized this beast and had Daedalus build the labyrinth to **ensure** that the beast would never escape.

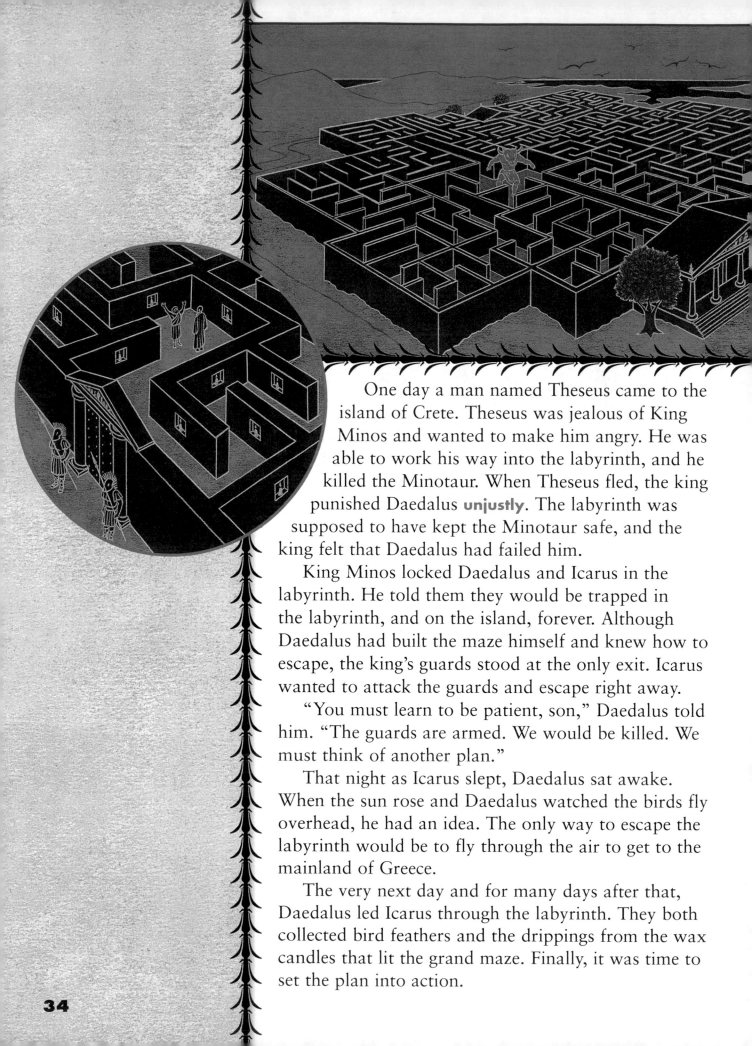

One day a man named Theseus came to the island of Crete. Theseus was jealous of King Minos and wanted to make him angry. He was able to work his way into the labyrinth, and he killed the Minotaur. When Theseus fled, the king punished Daedalus **unjustly**. The labyrinth was supposed to have kept the Minotaur safe, and the king felt that Daedalus had failed him.

King Minos locked Daedalus and Icarus in the labyrinth. He told them they would be trapped in the labyrinth, and on the island, forever. Although Daedalus had built the maze himself and knew how to escape, the king's guards stood at the only exit. Icarus wanted to attack the guards and escape right away.

"You must learn to be patient, son," Daedalus told him. "The guards are armed. We would be killed. We must think of another plan."

That night as Icarus slept, Daedalus sat awake. When the sun rose and Daedalus watched the birds fly overhead, he had an idea. The only way to escape the labyrinth would be to fly through the air to get to the mainland of Greece.

The very next day and for many days after that, Daedalus led Icarus through the labyrinth. They both collected bird feathers and the drippings from the wax candles that lit the grand maze. Finally, it was time to set the plan into action.

Daedalus started to work. He **fashioned** wings for himself and Icarus. He made the wings by sewing bird feathers together with fine thread. Then he sealed them with wax. It was difficult work, but at last, the wings were finished. Icarus demanded to try the wings right away.

"No," said Daedalus, "you will be careless, and you will ruin them. We must find a spot where we can catch a good wind that will carry us to safety."

Daedalus led Icarus up to the highest point of the labyrinth. There the father and son put on their wings. Before they took off, Daedalus gave his son a warning.

"Do not fly too close to the sun. The heat will melt the wax of your wings. Do not fly too close to the water. The dampness will weigh down your feathers. Be sure to keep a middle course. Follow me, and you will be safe."

Daedalus kissed his **beloved** son, and then the two soared into the sky. At first, Icarus **heeded** his father's warnings. But soon, the boy grew bored. He flapped his wings harder. The cool breeze felt wonderful on his face. The land and people below looked like no more than tiny specks. The thrill of flying was **exhilarating**, and soon Icarus had flown far ahead of his father.

"Icarus, you must slow down!" called Daedalus. "I warned you not to be foolish!"

35

But Icarus ignored him. *Surely nothing bad could happen to me in this beautiful sky*, thought Icarus. He continued to soar among the soft, **billowing** clouds. The warm rays of the sun felt wonderful. He decided to see how high he could fly.

Icarus climbed higher and higher into the sky. He did not notice how hot the sun was getting. He flew so high that he did not hear his father's calls.

"Icarus! Do not fly so close to the sun!" Daedalus cried. But it was no use. No answer came back to him. Soon Icarus had flown so high, his father could no longer see him.

Icarus soared onward and upward. He was lost in the joy of flight. By the time he noticed that the wax of his wings had begun to soften, it was too late. The wings loosened completely, and down, down, down Icarus went. He flapped his wings wildly, but it was no use. He disappeared into the sea.

Daedalus looked down into the water. He saw a few feathers floating on the surface and knew his son's fate. Icarus was lost in the waters that would from then on bear his name—the Icarian Sea.

At last, Daedalus arrived safely on land. But for as long as he lived, he **lamented** his son's stubborn nature. Now Icarus was gone. It was all because he had been impatient and never learned to listen.

THE SEVEN WONDERS OF TODAY'S WORLD

The Pyramids of Giza

The ancient Greeks and Romans made many different lists of man-made wonders of the world. Buildings and statues would qualify for the lists based on their size or another unusual quality. The most **renowned** list is now called the Seven Wonders of the Ancient World. All of those wonders were located in a small region around the Mediterranean Sea.

Today, many more amazing man-made wonders have been constructed all over the world. In the tradition of the Greeks and Romans, we can **compile** our own list of wonders that **span** the globe. These are wonders that we can visit today. Only one of the original seven ancient wonders still exists. A tour of today's wonders starts there, in the deserts of Egypt.

The Great Pyramid of Giza

The pyramids of Egypt were tombs for **pharaohs**. The largest pyramid was built at Giza, for Pharaoh Kuhfu. When it was completed in 2580 B.C., it was the tallest structure in the world. It held that record for nearly 4000 years. It is made up of over two million blocks of heavy limestone and granite. How did the ancient Egyptians build this massive structure without machines? No one knows for sure. However, most experts think the blocks were hauled up sloping ramps with ropes. Visitors from all over the world still flock to see this ancient wonder today.

The Great Wall of China

The Great Wall of China snakes through the mountains of northern China for more than 1500 miles (2414 kilometers). If it were in the U.S., it would stretch from Washington, D.C. to Denver, Colorado. The Great Wall is so large that it can even be seen from space.

The Great Wall started in different places as protection for different states. The individual sections were connected during the Qin (CHIN) Dynasty from 221–206 B.C. This tradition of connecting the wall lasted for centuries. Each dynasty added to the wall's height, length, and design.

During the Ming dynasty, from 1368–1644, the wall took on its present form. The brick work was enlarged and **sophisticated** designs were added. Many parts of the wall have been destroyed over the years. However, much of the wall has been restored, so visitors can still see this achievement.

The Great Wall of China

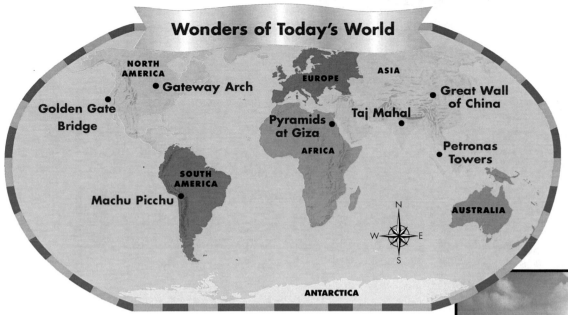

Wonders of Today's World

NORTH AMERICA

• Gateway Arch

Golden Gate Bridge

EUROPE

ASIA

Pyramids at Giza

Taj Mahal

Great Wall of China

AFRICA

Petronas Towers

SOUTH AMERICA

Machu Picchu

AUSTRALIA

ANTARCTICA

Machu Picchu

Machu Picchu (MAH choo PEEK choo) is the site of an ancient Inca city located in Peru on a mountain top. This ancient city is hidden between two larger peaks. Built between 1460 and 1470, Machu Picchu was remarkably intact when it was discovered in 1911 by an American explorer. This ancient city consists of stone buildings, walls, towers, and **terraces**. Everything is linked by a network of 3000 steps. This ancient city was entirely self-contained. The people of Machu Picchu did not have to travel outside of the city to find food and water. The terraces grew enough food to feed the population and fresh water flowed from natural springs.

Machu Picchu

The Taj Mahal

Taj Mahal

Many people consider the Taj Mahal in India to be the world's most beautiful building. An Indian emperor built it between 1632 and 1648 as a monument to his dead wife. It is actually a **mausoleum** that houses her grave. This spectacular monument is built entirely of white marble. **Symmetrical** towers frame the main building. Part of the monument's beauty is that it seems to change color. At dawn, it can appear pink. At night, it seems to glow in the moonlight.

39

The Golden Gate Bridge

The Golden Gate Bridge, located in San Francisco, California, has been **heralded** as one of the top construction achievements of the twentieth century.

The height of the towers reaches 746 feet (227 meters) above the water of the Golden Gate Strait. The total length of the bridge spans 8981 feet (2737 meters). The Golden Gate Bridge is known as one of the world's most beautiful bridges. It has tremendous towers, sweeping cables, and brilliant color. The bridge was ready for cars in 1938.

The Golden Gate Bridge

The Gateway Arch

Soaring 630 feet (192 meters) above the Mississippi River, the Gateway Arch in Saint Louis, Missouri is America's tallest human-made monument. The Gateway Arch is a memorial to Thomas Jefferson and to the historic role Saint Louis played as the gateway to the west. The construction of this astounding stainless steel arch was completed in 1965.

The Gateway Arch

Petronas Twin Towers

Petronas Twin Towers

Until 1998, the world's tallest skyscraper had always been in the United States. But that year, the Petronas Twin Towers in Kuala Lumpur, Malaysia, squeaked past Chicago's Sears Tower by 33 feet (10 meters). The **spires** on top of the Petronas Towers peak at an impressive 1483 feet (452 meters). The identical towers are linked by a bridge which creates a dramatic gateway to Kuala Lumpur. Other features of these towers include a curtain wall of glass and stainless steel sun shades. The shades are important because Malaysia is close to the equator where the sun's rays are the strongest.